EXPLORING WORLD CULTURES

Iraq

Ruth Bjorklund

Cavendish
Square

New York

Published in 2017 by Cavendish Square Publishing, LLC
243 5th Avenue, Suite 136, New York, NY 10016

First Edition

Website: cavendishsq.com

This publication represents the opinions and views of the author based on his or her personal experience, knowledge, and research. The information in this book serves as a general guide only. The author and publisher have used their best efforts in preparing this book and disclaim liability rising directly or indirectly from the use and application of this book.

CPSIA Compliance Information: Batch #CW17CSQ

All websites were available and accurate when this book was sent to press.

Cataloging-in-Publication Data

Names: Bjorklund, Ruth.
Title: Iraq / Ruth Bjorklund.
Description: New York : Cavendish Square Publishing, 2017. | Series: Exploring world cultures| Includes index. Identifiers: ISBN 9781502621573 (pbk.) | ISBN 9781502621597 (library bound) | ISBN 9781502621580 (6 pack) | ISBN 9781502621603 (ebook)
Subjects: LCSH: Iraq--Juvenile literature.
Classification: LCC DS70.62 B56 2017 | DDC 956.7--dc23

Editorial Director: David McNamara
Editor: Kristen Susienka
Copy Editor: Rebecca Rohan
Associate Art Director: Amy Greenan
Designer: Joseph Macri
Production Coordinator: Karol Szymczuk
Photo Research: J8 Media

The photographs in this book are used by permission and through the courtesy of: Cover, pp. 5, 18, 28 Jane Sweeney/Lonely Planet Images/Getty Images; p. 6 Artyom Ernst/Shutterstock.com; p. 7 Michael Runkel/ RobertHarding/Getty Images; p. 8 Werner Forman/Universal Images Group/Getty Images; p. 10 Ahamad Al-Rubaye/AFP/Getty Images; p. 11 Stockbyte/Getty Images; p. 12 AFP/Getty Images; p. 13 Anton Ivanov/ Shutterstock.com; p. 14 Ramzi Haidar/AFP/Getty Images; p. 16 Eric Lafforgue/ArabianEye/Getty Images; p. 20 Sadik Gulec/Shutterstock.com; p. 22©Epa European Pressphoto Agency b.v./Alamy Stock Photo; p. 24 DEA/Archivo J. Lange/De Agostini/Getty Images; p. 25 Anadolu Agency/Getty Images; p. 26 STR/AFP/Getty Images; p. 27 ©AP Images; p. 29 Sabah Arar/AFP/Getty Images.

Printed in the United States of America

Contents

Introduction

Iraq is a country in the Middle East. People have lived in Iraq for many centuries. Long ago, Iraq was an ancient area called Mesopotamia. Early people invented many important things, such as writing and the wheel.

The people of Iraq are called Iraqis. Today most people live in big cities, but there are many farms and villages, too.

Different groups of people, called tribes, call Iraq home. Some tribes are small, and other tribes have more than one million people.

Iraq has deserts, mountains, hills, rivers, and valleys. Lots of animals, birds, and fish live there. Many types of trees, shrubs, and grasses grow in Iraq.

A group of Iraqi schoolchildren is eager to start the day.

In some areas, there is war and fighting. But Iraqis make time to gather together for music, food, and holiday celebrations. Let's take a look at the colorful history, culture, and people of Iraq.

Geography

Iraq is part of West Asia, North Africa, and the Middle East. Iraq has a tiny coastline. It is almost completely surrounded by land. Southern Iraq is desert. In the northeast, there are mountains.

Gazelles live in Iraq's deserts and grasslands.

The Tigris and Euphrates Rivers flow across Iraq. Fish, birds, and ducks make homes there. Many animals, such as hyenas and foxes, live in the hills and plains. Lizards and snakes live in the desert.

The highest mountain
in Iraq is Cheekha Dar.
It is 11,848 feet
(3,611 meters) tall.

Mt. Cheekha Dar is
snow-capped all year.

Iraq has two seasons, summer and winter. Summer is warm, and skies are clear. The desert is hot and dry. Temperatures are milder in the mountains and plains. Rain falls in winter. Some areas have more rain than others. Snow falls on the mountains.

Built for Speed

Endangered cheetahs live in Iraq. They run faster than any other animal.

Hundreds of years ago, Iraq was called Mesopotamia. Many different civilizations lived there. Each civilization built inventions. The ancient Sumerians invented the wheel, writing, and the number system we use to

Ancient Sumerians wrote on slabs of stone.

measure time. Early rulers built the cities of Babylon and Baghdad, and Iraq became a world center for learning, culture, and trade.

Later, civilizations like the Romans, Greeks, Muslims, and Ottoman Turks ruled Iraq. The Ottoman Empire ruled until Britain took control after World War I. Iraq gained independence in 1932.

In the 1980s and 1990s, a man named Saddam Hussein led Iraq into many wars. He was a strict ruler called a dictator. In 2003, some governments thought Iraq was hiding weapons. Saddam Hussein was captured. Without a leader, Iraqi groups started fighting each other and the foreign armies. Violent terrorist groups also invaded Iraq. Today, battles continue, but hopeful Iraqis elected a new government in 2014.

A Rich Land

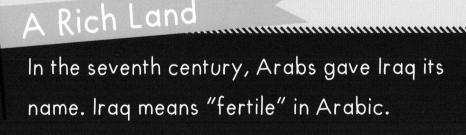

In the seventh century, Arabs gave Iraq its name. Iraq means "fertile" in Arabic.

Government

The official name of Iraq is the Republic of Iraq. People vote for their leaders. Lawmakers wrote Iraq's **constitution** in 2005.

The Council of Representatives at work

Iraq's government is divided into three branches: executive, legislative, and judicial. The president heads the executive branch. There are three vice presidents and a prime minister. The prime minister is the head of government and chooses a council of ministers.

The legislative branch is known as the Council of Representatives. There are 328 members. They make the country's laws.

One-sixth of Iraqis live in the capital city of Baghdad.

The highest courts in Iraq's judicial branch are the Supreme Court and the Court of Cassation. Other courts are a court of appeals and the juvenile, religious, and criminal courts.

The Colors of the Flag

Iraq's flag has three stripes: black, red, and white. The black symbolizes war, the red means bloody struggle, and the white means hope.

The Iraqi flag waves in the breeze.

The Economy

War has hurt Iraq's **economy**, but Iraqis are hardworking. In cities, some Iraqis are teachers, technology workers, bankers, doctors, businessmen, and lawyers. Others are cooks, maids, taxi drivers, and oil and construction workers.

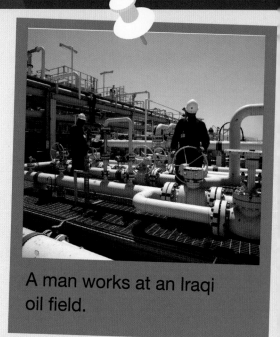

A man works at an Iraqi oil field.

There is rich farmland in Iraq. Farmers grow wheat, rice, corn, dates, figs, grapes, and cotton. People also raise goats, sheep, and chickens. They sell milk, eggs, meat, leather, and wool.

Iraq has one-fifth of the world's oil.

Iraq has many natural resources, like oil. Oil was discovered in Iraq in 1927. Most of Iraq's wealth comes from selling oil to other countries. Other natural resources are salt, stone, and natural gas.

Palm trees are on the 50-dinar note.

Iraq manufactures chemicals, textiles, leather, and metal products.

Money

Iraqi money is called dinar. The largest is a 25,000-dinar note. It shows a Kurdish farmer on the front and Hammurabi's code of laws on the back.

Iraq has many environmental problems. Cars, trucks, and factories dirty the air in cities. Dirty water from houses, roads, and factories runs into rivers, lakes, and the sea.

Dirty water can harm crops.

Iraq has many oil wells. Workers use chemicals to pump oil and natural gas out of the ground. The chemicals kill fish, birds, and animals. Iraq also has environmental problems because of war. Dangerous chemicals from weapons poison the soil and water.

A Special Fish

The endangered Iraqi blind barb is a cave-dwelling fish found only in Iraq. Dirty water is destroying its home.

Iraq has a variety of fish, birds, reptiles, and mammals. Some are endangered, such as cheetahs and gazelles. Iraq's government is making laws to clean the environment and protect wildlife.

FACT!

The Mesopotamia Marsh is a vast wetland in Iraq. It was destroyed by Saddam Hussein. Today, Iraqis are restoring the marsh. Hundreds of different birds, fish, and ducks live there.

More than thirty-four million people live in Iraq. Most people live in the large cities of Baghdad, Basra, Mosul, Erbil, and Kirkuk. Nearly everyone lives near the Euphrates and Tigris Rivers.

Women dance together at a celebration.

Between 75 and 80 percent of Iraqis are Arabs. Arabs are people who speak Arabic and whose **ancestors** came from West Asia and North Africa. Most Iraqi Arabs are light-skinned with brown eyes and brown hair, but some have blue or green eyes and light hair.

Tribal leaders are called sheiks.

Between 15 and 20 percent of Iraqis are Kurdish. The Kurdish region has its own prime minister, flag, national anthem, and army. Turkmen and Assyrians are other Iraqi groups. Each group has their own language and customs.

Khams

Iraqi Arab tribes are divided into smaller groups, called clans and khams. A kham is a family group based on all the male children who share the same great-great-grandfather.

Lifestyle

Many children live with their parents, aunts, uncles, cousins, and grandparents. As families grow, more rooms are added onto the family house.

An Iraqi family is ready to enjoy a meal.

Women cook, clean, and raise the children. Men work outside of the house. Many men are soldiers now, so more women have jobs such as teachers, doctors, and factory workers.

Most children go to school from ages six to eleven. Many go until age fifteen. More boys than girls go to high school. Many children in poor

Families and Children

Iraq's government wants each family to have at least five children.

families stop going to school at a young age and have jobs.

Parents teach their children many **values**. A good child is loyal to family, tribe, and country. Parents share their values about love, kindness, generosity, religion, and respect for others.

FACT!

If getting married, nearly all brides and grooms belong to the same tribe.

There are many different religions celebrated in Iraq. Ninety-seven percent of Iraqis are Muslim, including most Kurds. The Muslim religion is called Islam. There are two branches of Islam, Sunni and Shiite.

Many mosques have domed roofs and a tower.

Muslims follow the teachings of the Prophet Muhammad. Muhammad worried that people were too greedy. He prayed for them and said Allah, his god, wanted him to preach Islam. Muslims follow rules called the Five Pillars of Islam. They are: reciting "There is no god but Allah and Muhammad is his messenger"; praying five times a day; giving

money to the poor; fasting during the holy month of **Ramadan**; and making a journey to Mecca, Muhammad's birthplace.

There are other religions in Iraq, too, such as Christianity and Judaism. They are not always treated well. Today, many non-Muslims are being pushed out of Iraq or choose to leave to seek a better life.

A Religious Journey

The journey to Mecca is called the hajj.

Language

There are more than three hundred million Arabic speakers in the world. Nearly all Iraqis speak Arabic. Other languages are Kurdish, Turkmen, Farsi, Russian, Hebrew, and Urdu. The constitution lets children learn in their first language as well as Arabic. Kurdish is the second-most spoken

In Iraq, students begin school at age six.

FACT!

Arabic storytellers have been writing stories and poems since ancient times. Two famous stories are "Ali Baba and the Forty Thieves" and "Aladdin and the Magic Lamp."

language in Iraq. Arabic and Kurdish are Iraq's two official languages.

There are twenty-eight letters in the Arabic alphabet. People read right to left. Arabic writing uses special marks, such as dots, over the letters. Most written words do not use vowels. Vowels are used only when speaking.

Arabic Words Today

There are many words English speakers use that come from Arabic. Some are: acrobat, algebra, candy, chemistry, guitar, mummy, soda, and zero.

Arts and Festivals

Ancient Iraqis made pottery, sculptures, and jewelry. They created paintings of battles and royalty. Today, artists paint or use gemstones and clay tiles to make patterns and designs. These patterns are called mosaics. Mosaics

Mosaics like this are popular in Iraqi architecture.

decorate walls, pathways, and buildings, especially mosques. Other crafts are rug-making and woodcarving.

FACT!

Iraqi musical instruments are the oud, lute (string instruments), drums, and tambourine.

For celebrations such as weddings and the New Year, Iraqis enjoy special foods, music, and dancing. For religious holidays, Iraqis pray together with family and friends. Eid al-Fitr is a

In Erbil, Iraq, people celebrate Persian New Year with fireworks.

three-day holiday at the end of the holy month of Ramadan. During Ramadan, people do not eat between sunrise and sunset. Afterwards, Iraqis gather with friends and family, eat sweets, wear new clothes, give gifts, and decorate their homes with lights.

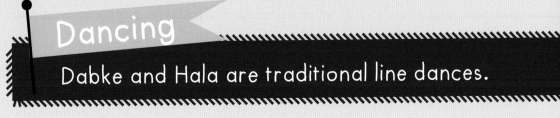

Dancing

Dabke and Hala are traditional line dances.

25

Fun and Play

Iraqis are hardworking people, and many suffer from the effects of war. But Iraqis have a lot of spirit. Adults and children all want to enjoy some fun. People, mostly boys, play soccer, also called football, in dusty fields and streets. Soccer

The National Iraqi soccer team

is the national sport. The Iraqi national team has done well in the World Cup and the Olympics.

FACT!

Many Iraqi families love picnics.

It is not traditional for girls to play sports, but today, there are many girls' and women's

basketball teams. At first, playing sports was so new to Iraqi girls that many had to learn how to run before learning how to shoot a ball through a hoop.

Iraqi girls playing soccer

In dangerous areas, many parents keep their children indoors. To stay safe, many Iraqi children play indoors with video games and dice.

Ancient Games

Since ancient times, Iraqis have played chess and backgammon.

Food

Iraqi food is sweet-smelling and delicious. Iraqis cook with many fruits and vegetables and meat such as lamb, beef, and chicken.

An everyday meal is soup, rice, lentils, and kebabs. To make a kebab, cooks mix

Pastries are filled with nuts and spices.

spices and ground meat and slide the mixture onto a stick. Many meals are cooked outside over an open fire. Meals are served with yogurt, raisins, nuts, and flatbread.

Beekeeping

For five thousand years, Iraqis have been beekeepers. Honey is a popular food.

During the Ramadan fast, people wake early for a meal of dates, grains, and bananas. After sunset, they have a small meal and juice. When Ramadan ends, Iraqis start Eid al-Fitr with a breakfast of cream, honey, and bread. Later, families and friends gather to feast on rich meat dishes and pastries; cookies; and cakes made with dates, figs, nuts, butter, and sugar.

An Iraqi street stand sells pomegranate juice.

Many Iraqis' favorite fruit juice is pomegranate juice.

29

Glossary

ancestors Family members from whom a person has descended.

constitution A document that describes a country's laws.

economy A country's system of making and selling goods and services.

endangered At risk of dying off.

Ramadan A sacred month for Muslims, during which they eat little food and reflect on their lives.

values Things people consider important, like family, friendship, and kindness.

worship To pay honor or respect to a divine being or supernatural power.

Find Out More

Books

Apte, Sunita. *Mesopotamia*. New York: Children's
Press, 2010.

Blesch, Will. *Understanding Iraq Today*. Hockessin,
DE: Mitchell Lane Publishers, 2015.

Websites

Ancient Mesopotamia

http://mesopotamia.mrdonn.org

Islam for Kids

http://islamkids.org

Videos

Debka Dance

https://youtu.be/YMk8XtMRcPE

This video shows a traditional Arabic folk dance
popular in Iraq.

Index

About the Author

Ruth Bjorklund has written many books for young people. She lives on an island near Seattle, Washington. She likes boating, reading, and visiting other countries.